LOST
IN
CABO

Written and Illustrated

By

Sue Bee Balentine

This book is dedicated to my children

Heather, Taylor, and Connor

Whom have given me more inspiration

Than they will ever know

I Love You

Mom

A special thanks goes out to

Mark Swann

For believing in me

Through and through

This is the story about a shy little boy and a sad little dog. Connor is a young boy who loves to spend time in his room and rarely goes outside to play. Every year Connor´s parents enjoy going to Mexico for their vacation. Normally Connor dreads this trip, but one year something very special happened.

Trips to Mexico were always filled with beautiful scenery and yummy food. Connor always felt like he was tagging along and wishing he was in his room.

Connor´s room was filled with lots of entertaining and amusing things to do, but his room was not in Mexico.

One day while Connor was taking a stroll with his parents, he saw something in the street. It was a sad little dog.

As soon as the little dog saw Connor, he became overjoyed. With his tail wagging, he ran straight to Connor without a thought.

Connor and the little dog immediately knew that they were meant to be together. They fell in love at first sight.

"Can I keep him mom? Can I keep him dad? Please?
Please? Please?" Connor begged, and so did the little dog.

"He may be lost or have an owner!", exclaimed Connor´s mother.

"We must first take him to the animal shelter", said Connor's father.

Connor's father explained that the animal shelter is a place people can take animals to be rescued. Sometimes a person may find their lost pet at the shelter, or animals live there when they don't have a home. When an animal at the shelter does not have a home, they can be adopted by a family that does. Animal shelters are a wonderful sanctuary and safe place to be.

Connor still did not want to take the little dog to the shelter; he did not want to leave him. Connor felt sad and blue, but he decided to name the little dog Pedro.

The workers at the animal shelter were very polite and assured Connor they would take very good care of Pedro.

Pedro was very stinky! "Peeeeeeuuuuuu!" Connor heard the worker cry. The first thing that Pedro got at the animal shelter was a bath.

Every day Pedro went for a walk, sometimes a volunteer would take him.
Pedro was always watching for Connor,

but he never came.

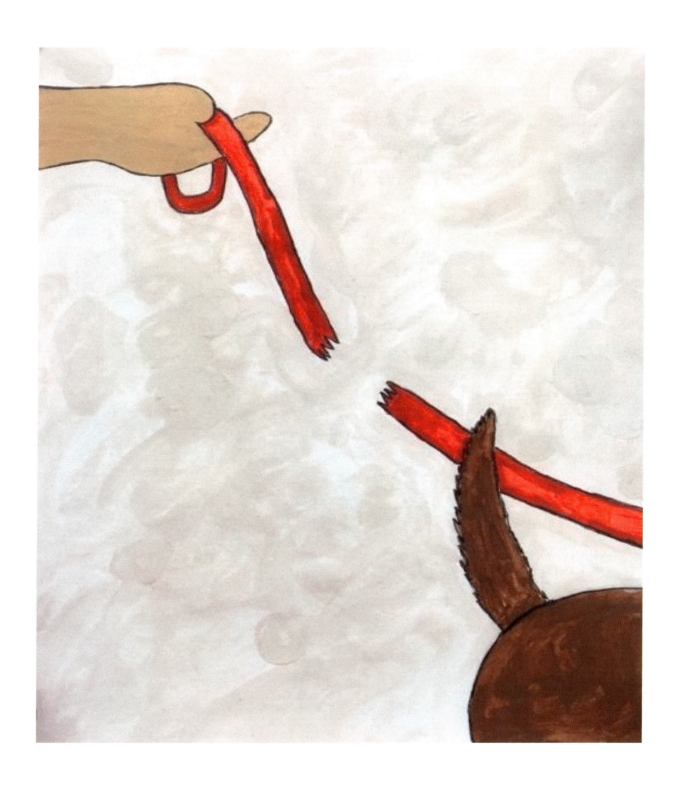

One day Pedro got a brilliant idea! He decided while out on his walk he would break his leash, run away, and go find Connor… and that's exactly what he did!

The very same day that Pedro ran away something terrible happened! Connor showed up at the animal shelter to see if he was there! "Is Pedro here?" asked Connor. "No", said the worker, "he ran that way."

"Oh no!," cried Connor, "I must find him!" Connor took off running as fast as he could!

The first place Connor decided to look was the marina, but Pedro was not there.

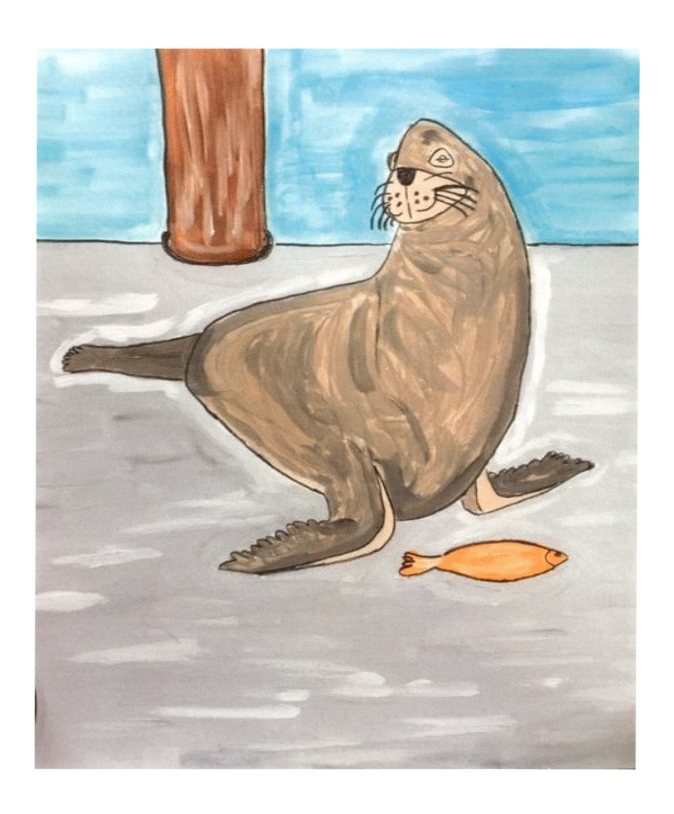

The only one there was "Pancho" the sea lion.

The next place Connor decided to look was the Cabo Cantina, but Pedro was not there either, only a couple of locals.

Then Connor got a bright idea and decided to go look at the first place he found Pedro. He was not there either.

Connor burst into tears, "Where could Pedro be? He has to be somewhere." Connor was so determined to find Pedro that he decided to look one more place. He ran all the way to the ocean!

And there he was!

Pedro ran straight to Connor and jumped into his arms! They finally found each other. They were together at last.

"Mom! Dad! Pedro must not have an owner! Can we adopt him? Please? Please? Please?" pleaded Connor. "Yes, we can adopt Pedro and take him home," said Connor's parents joyfully.

That trip to Mexico changed a young boy and a sad little dog. Connor did not spend much time in his room anymore. He found something more special to entertain and amuse him. He took Pedro for walks every day, and this time Pedro did not want to run away. From that day on Pedro and Connor were never alone again.

In 2015 we performed over 3,450 spay and neuter surgeries, facilitated over 400 adoptions and presented our Animal Awareness Educational Program to thousands of school children and families. Last year alone, we took in and cared for over 3000 animals

info@Loscaboshumanesociety.com

Made in the USA
Lexington, KY
14 March 2017